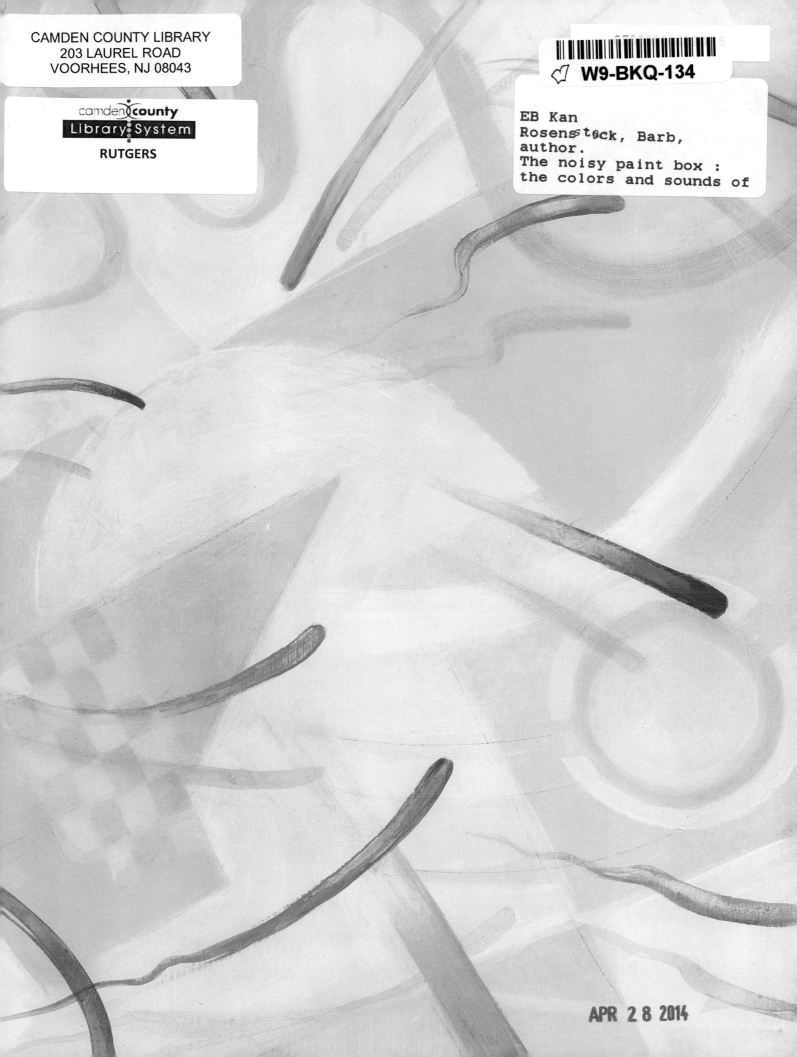

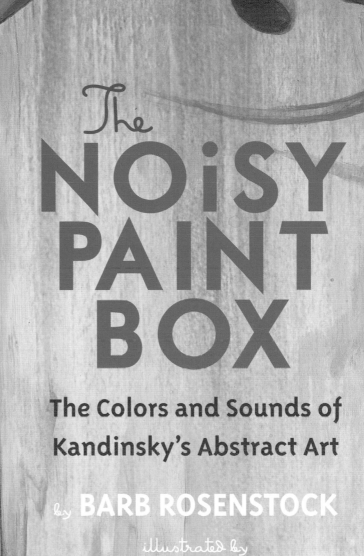

The NOiSY PAINT BOX

The Colors and Sounds of Kandinsky's Abstract Art

by **BARB ROSENSTOCK**

illustrated by

MARY GRANDPRÉ

Alfred A. Knopf

NEW YORK

For Mr. Paul Forneh, the best teacher ever.
Thank you, wherever you are.
—B. R.
For all young artists who look and listen
with brave hearts
—M. G.

$\mathcal{V}$asya Kandinsky spent his days learning to be a proper Russian boy.

He studied bookfuls of math, science, and history.

He practiced
piano scales
to the marching
click of the
M E T R O N O M E.

He sat stiff and straight at
dressed-up dinners while the
grown-ups
talked
and talked,
and
talked.

Vasya's well-off world was
perfectly polite . . . until the day
his aunt gave him a small wooden
paint box.

"Every proper Russian boy should appreciate art," said Auntie. She showed Vasya the correct way to mix colors on the paint-box palette.

Vasya mixed red with yellow; then he mixed red with blue.

As the colors changed, Vasya heard a *whisper.* HISS!

Louder. HISS!

Then louder still. HISS!

"What's that sound?" asked Vasya.

"I don't hear a thing," said Auntie.

Vasya listened as his brush stirred and swished.
The swirling colors trilled like an orchestra tuning up
for a magical symphony.

"Mama! Papa!" called Vasya. "What a noisy paint box!"

"Silly Vasily!" said Papa.

"Stop being foolish!" said Mama.

Vasya painted the sound of the colors.

He spun a bright lemon circle onto the canvas. It clinked like the highest notes on the keyboard. He brushed a powerful navy rectangle that vibrated deeply like the lowest cello strings. He tossed up jagged swashes of blaring crimson and added cheerful dots of burbling green, clanging orange, and tinkling violet. Vasya painted and painted until the colors went

quiet.

"Look what I made!"
shouted Vasya.
"Is it a house?" asked Auntie.
"Is it a flower?" asked Mama.
"What's it supposed to *be*?"
asked Papa.
"It's music!" said Vasya,
waltzing his painting
around the house.

"Calm down!" said Mama.

"Do some math!" said Papa.

"Heavens!" said Auntie. "This boy
needs a proper art class."

So Vasya went to art
class and learned to draw
houses and flowers—
just like everyone else.

As the years passed, Vasya finished school and studied to be a lawyer. He ignored his noisy paint box and lived the way people expected.

But Vasya couldn't ignore the sounds of the colors singing to him in the streets of Moscow.

The canary-colored mailbox whistling as he rode to work.

The scarlet sunset haze ringing above the ancient Kremlin walls.

An ivory chorus of snowflakes
scattered on the sable collar
of his overcoat.

One evening, suitably steamed and starched, Vasya attended
the opera. As the orchestra's music crashed around him,
the colors of the noisy paint box twirled wildly in his mind.
Stomping lines of vermilion and coral. Caroling triangles in
pistachio and garnet. Thundering arches of aqua and ebony,
with shrill points of cobalt and saffron.

Vasya *heard* the colors singing.
Vasya *saw* the music dancing.

And Vasya was never quite as proper again.

He quit his job teaching law and moved from Moscow to Munich to be a painter. He studied with *this* famous teacher, then *that* one.

"Is it a house?"

"Is it a flower?"

"What's it supposed to *be*?" his teachers asked.

Vasya wanted to paint the colors he heard, but maybe the famous teachers knew best. Once again, Vasya put houses and flowers, animals and people into his paintings, just like everyone expected. The teachers were happy.

Vasya was not.

His artist friends understood. They too were
tired of painting pretty landscapes and pretty
ladies. They thought art needed to change.

"Art should make you feel," Vasya told them.
"Like music."

"Exactly!" said his friends. But none of
them knew how to paint feelings . . .

until the day Vasya grew brave enough . . .

and invited the world to see the paintings
roaring from his noisy paint box.

Snapping cerulean points. Crunching crimson squares. Whispering charcoal lines. Vasya named these paintings after the music he loved: *Improvisation, Composition, Accompaniment, Fugue, Movement,* and simply, *Three Sounds.*

With his noisy paint box, Vasya Kandinsky created something entirely new—

        abstract art.

It took a long time for people to understand.

"Is it a house?" "Is it a flower?"

"What's it supposed to *be*?"

"It's my art," Vasya answered.

"How does

it make

you feel?"

Author's Note

Vasily Kandinsky was born in Moscow, Russia, on December 4, 1866. His father, also named Vasily, was a wealthy tea merchant, and his mother, Lidia, was a noblewoman with a passion for music. Vasily (or Vasya, as he was sometimes called) traveled with his family to Italy and then to Odessa, Russia, on the shore of the Black Sea, for his father's health. When he was five, his parents divorced, and Vasya lived with his aunt Elizabeth while finishing school. He attended law school in Moscow, then taught law and economics as an adult.

This book is historical fiction. The dialogue is imagined, although the events are true. In his writings, Kandinsky describes hearing a hissing sound as a child when he first mixed colors in the paint box his aunt gave him. He continued experiencing colors as sounds, and sounds as colors, throughout his life. It's thought that Kandinsky probably had a harmless genetic condition called synesthesia (sih-nuhs-*thee*-zhuh), although accurate tests to detect it weren't invented during his lifetime. In people with synesthesia, one sense triggers a different sense, allowing them, for example, to hear colors, see music, taste words, or smell numbers. Scientists believe those with synesthesia may have more pathways between the sense areas in the brain or that their senses communicate in ways other people's do not. There are at least sixty different types of synesthesia, and it's estimated to occur in one out of every five thousand individuals.

As an adult, Kandinsky attended an exhibition of Claude Monet's *Haystacks*. The paintings stunned him; it was the first time he saw art that was not realistic, and he never forgot the experience. Later, at a performance of Richard Wagner's opera *Lohengrin,* he saw wild shapes and colors in his mind as the music played. At thirty, Kandinsky established himself as an artist in Germany. He was a

Painting with Green Center, 1913. 108.9 x 118.4 cm.
Art Institute of Chicago.

White Zig Zag, 1922. 95 x 125 cm.
Galleria d'Arte Moderna di Ca' Pesaro, Venice, Italy.

Improvisation VII (Composition VII), 1913. 200 x 300 cm.
State Tretyakov Gallery, Moscow, Russia.

Two Ovals, 1919. 107 x 89.5 cm.
Russian State Museum, St. Petersburg, Russia.

founder of the influential art group the Blue Rider and he later taught at the world-renowned Bauhaus school. In 1910, he painted his first completely abstract painting, which sparked a revolution in the art world.

After a long, successful life as a painter, Vasily Kandinsky died on December 13, 1944, in Neuilly-sur-Seine, France. Large collections of his art hang at the Guggenheim Museum and the Museum of Modern Art in New York City, the Art Institute of Chicago, Musée National d'Art Moderne in Paris, the Städtische Galerie in Munich, the State Tretyakov Gallery in Moscow, and many other museums around the world.

Maybe someday you will go and hear them.

Painting with Green Center © 2013 Artists Rights Society (ARS), New York/ADAGP, Paris. Photo credit: Album/Art Resource, NY.

White Zig Zag © 2013 Artists Rights Society (ARS), New York/ADAGP, Paris. Photo credit: Scala/Art Resource, NY.

Two Ovals © 2013 Artists Rights Society (ARS), New York/ADAGP, Paris. Photo credit: Scala/Art Resource, NY.

Improvisation VII (Composition VII) © 2013 Artists Rights Society (ARS), New York/ADAGP, Paris. Photo credit: Erich Lessing/Art Resource, NY.

Sources:

Barnett, Vivian Endicott, et al. *Kandinsky at the Guggenheim*. New York. Guggenheim Museum Publications, 2009.

Grohmann, Will. *Wassily Kandinsky: Life and Work*. New York: Abrams, 1958.

Kandinsky, Wassily. *Concerning the Spiritual in Art*. New York: Dover Publications, 1977, 1914.

Kandinsky, Wassily. *Point and Line to Plane*. New York: Dover Publications, 1979, 1947.

Kandinsky, Wassily. *Sounds*. New Haven: Yale University Press, 1981.

Kandinsky, Wassily, Kenneth C. Lindsay, and Peter Vergo. *Kandinsky: Complete Writings on Art*. Boston: G. K. Hall, 1982. (The quotations on *The Noisy Paint Box* end pages and jacket were taken from Kandinsky's essay "Reminiscences," which is in this collection.)

Marc, Franz. *The Blaue Reiter Almanac*. New York: Viking Press, 1974.

Rapelli, Paola. *Kandinsky*. New York: Dorling Kindersley, 1999.

Ward, Ossian. "The Man Who Heard His Paintbox Hiss." *Telegraph* (London), June 10, 2006.

Weiss, Peg. *Kandinsky and Old Russia: The Artist as Ethnographer and Shaman*. New Haven: Yale University Press, 1995.

For more information about Kandinsky and synesthesia, visit the following websites:

guggenheim.org (search word: Kandinsky)

wassilykandinsky.net

faculty.washington.edu/chudler/syne.html

pbs.org/wgbh/nova/secretlife/scientists/steffie-tomson

THIS IS A BORZOI BOOK PUBLISHED BY ALFRED A. KNOPF

Text copyright © 2014 by Barb Rosenstock
Jacket art and interior illustrations copyright © 2014 by Mary GrandPré

All rights reserved. Published in the United States by Alfred A. Knopf, an imprint of
Random House Children's Books, a division of Random House, Inc., New York.

Knopf, Borzoi Books, and the colophon are registered trademarks of Random House, Inc.

Visit us on the Web! randomhouse.com/kids

Educators and librarians, for a variety of teaching tools, visit us at
RHTeachersLibrarians.com

Library of Congress Cataloging-in-Publication Data
Rosenstock, Barbara.
The noisy paint box : The colors and sounds of Kandinsky's abstract art / by Barb Rosenstock ;
illustrated by Mary GrandPré. — 1st ed.
p. cm.
"This is a borzoi book."
ISBN 978-0-307-97848-6 (trade) — ISBN 978-0-307-97849-3 (lib. bdg.) — ISBN 978-0-307-97850-9 (ebook)
[1. Kandinsky, Wassily, 1866—1944—Juvenile literature. 2. Artists—Russia (Federation)—Biography—
Juvenile literature.]
I. GrandPré, Mary, illustrator. II. Title.
N6999.K33R67 2014
759.7—dc23
[B]
2012032800

The text of this book is set in Horley Old-Style, Masana Script, and Triplex Sans.
The illustrations were created using acrylic paint and paper collage.

MANUFACTURED IN MALAYSIA
February 2014
10 9 8 7 6 5 4 3 2 1

First Edition

"I let myself go. I had little thought for houses and trees,
drawing colored lines and blobs on the canvas with my
palette knife, making them sing just as powerfully as
I knew how." —Vasily Kandinsky

"I could hear the hiss of the colors as they mingled." -V.K.